1st Recital Series

Including works of:
- James Curnow
- Craig Alan
- Mike Hannickel
- Ann Lindsay

FOR Bb TENOR SAXOPHONE

Solos for Beginning
through Early Intermediate
level musicians

CURNOW® MUSIC

EXCLUSIVELY DISTRIBUTED BY

HAL•LEONARD® CORPORATION

7777 W. BLUEMOUND RD. P.O. BOX 13819 MILWAUKEE, WI 53213

T0050713

Edition Number: CMP 0847.03

1st Recital Series
Solos for Beginning through Early Intermediate level musicians
Bb Tenor Saxophone

ISBN: 978-90-431-1910-8

CD Accompaniment tracks performed by Becky Shaw

CD number: 19.042-3 CMP

Foreword

High quality solo/recital literature that is appropriate for performers playing at the Beginner through Early Intermediate skill levels is finally here! Each of the **1st RECITAL SERIES** books is loaded with exciting and varied solo pieces that have been masterfully composed or arranged for your instrument.

Included with the solo book is a professionally recorded CD that demonstrates each piece. Use these examples to help develop proper performance practices. There is also a recording of the accompaniment alone that can be used for performance (and rehearsal) when a live accompanist is not available. A separate Piano Accompaniment book is available [edition nr. CMP 0859.03].

Table of Contents

Track   Page

1   Tuning Note B♭ Concert

2 **3**   And All This Jazz 5

4 **5**   Declaration. 6

6 **7**   Memoir 7

8 **9**   Locomotion 8

10 **11**   The Matador 9

12 **13**   To A Wild Rose 10

14 **15**   Waltz 11

16 **17**   Swing Low 12

18 **19**   Minuet 13

20 **21**   Divergents 14

22 **23**   Slavonic Dance. 15

24 **25**   Serenade 16

☐   *Solo with accompaniment*

■   *Accompaniment*

1. AND ALL THIS JAZZ

Craig Alan (ASCAP)

Copyright © 2003 by **Curnow Music Press, Inc.**

2. DECLARATION

James Curnow (ASCAP)

Bb TENOR SAXOPHONE

Bb TENOR SAXOPHONE

3. MEMOIR

Ann Lindsay (ASCAP)

Copyright © 2003 by **Curnow Music Press, Inc.**

4. LOCOMOTION

James Curnow (ASCAP)

5. THE MATADOR

Mike Hannickel (ASCAP)

Habanera tempo (♩=108)

Edward MacDowell
6. TO A WILD ROSE
Arr. **James Curnow** (ASCAP)

Copyright © 2003 by **Curnow Music Press, Inc.**

Johannes Brahms
7. WALTZ

Arr. **James Curnow** (ASCAP)

8. SWING LOW

Arr. **Mike Hannickel** (ASCAP)

Johann Sebastian Bach
9. MINUET

Arr. **James Curnow** (ASCAP)

Bb TENOR SAXOPHONE

10. DIVERGENTS

James Curnow (ASCAP)

Moderately fast with energy (♩ = 96)

14

Track

Antonin Dvorak
11. SLAVONIC DANCE
Opus 72, #3

Arr. **James Curnow** (ASCAP)

B♭ TENOR SAXOPHONE

Franz Joseph Haydn

12. SERENADE
Opus 3, No. 5

Bb TENOR SAXOPHONE

Arr. **James Curnow** (ASCAP)

Moderately slow, in a singing style (♩ = 88)

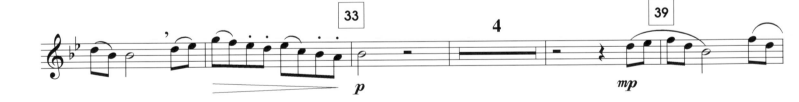

Rall.

TABLE OF CONTENTS

	Page		Page
Austrian Hymn	54	Jock O' Hazeldean	32
Ballad Of King Henry, The	28	Joseph And Mary	14
Bells Of London, The	10	Leezie Lindsay	42
Bergerette	34	Little Jack Horner	6
Beside Thy Cradle Here I Stand	56	London Bridge Is Falling Down	4
Bohemian Dance	24	Luther's Hymn	20
Bohemian Song	18	Minuet	12
Canon In A Minor	30	My Country, 'Tis Of Thee	12
Cashmere Song	14	Nineteen Birds	16
Chimes, The	44	North Wind Doth Blow, The	38
Christ Was Born On Christmas Day	50	Now The Sun Is Sinking	4
Christmas Song	8	Old French Air	16
Cradle-Song	48	Parting Song	36
Creole Song	40	Plaisir d'Amour	22
Cruel Rose, The	24	Polish Dance	44
Day Of Christmas, The	46	Rose Is Red, The	6
Ding Dong Bell	4	Russian Hymn	26
Dutch Tune	34	Scale Of D	20
Evening	6	Schubert Waltz	52
Exaudet's Minuet	48	Seagull, The	26
First Noël, The	22	Sleep, Belovèd, Sleep	46
Four And Twenty Blackbirds	10	Spring Song	52
Frère Jacques	28	Sulky Sue	2
Giroflè, Giroflà	18	Swing Song	2
Happy New Year	12	There Was An Old Woman, As I've Heard Tell	36
Hippity Hop!	40	To Market	2
Holy Night	50	What Tongue Can Tell Thy Greatness, Lord?	58
Hot Cross Buns	38	Winter	54
Hush-A-Bye Baby	8	Winter, Farewell	38
If I Were A Tiny Elfin	6	Wraggle-Taggle Gipsies, The	30
Irish Tune	44		

First Duet Book

SECONDO

Swing Song

To Market

Sulky Sue

First Duet Book

PRIMO

Swing Song

Andante con moto

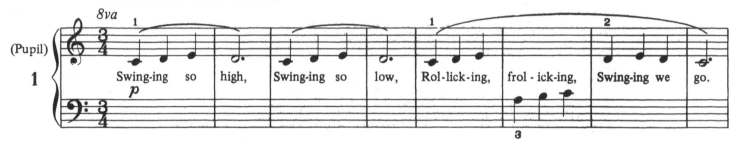

Swing-ing so high, Swing-ing so low, Rol-lick-ing, frol-ick-ing, Swing-ing we go.

Fast-er we fly, Wind rush-es by, Rol-lick-ing, frol-ick-ing, Up to the sky.

To Market

Andantino

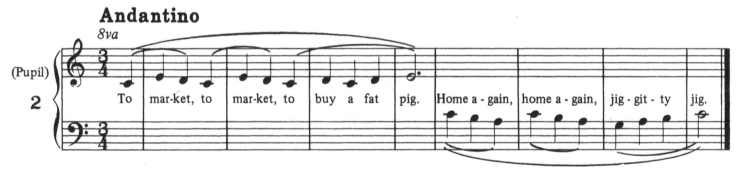

To mar-ket, to mar-ket, to buy a fat pig. Home a-gain, home a-gain, jig-git-ty jig.

Sulky Sue

Andante

Here's Sul-ky Sue, What shall we do? Turn her face to-wards the wall, 'till she comes to!

48574

SECONDO

Ding-Dong, Bell

Andante

London Bridge Is Falling Down

Allegro

English Folk Tune

(Pupil)
5

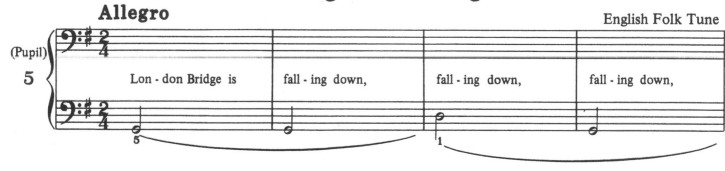

Lon - don Bridge is | fall - ing down, | fall - ing down, | fall - ing down,

Lon - don Bridge is | fall - ing down, | My fair | La - dy.

Now the Sun Is Sinking

Andante

(Pupil)
6

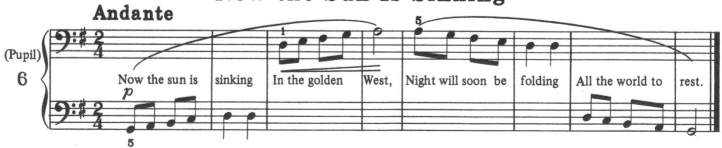

Now the sun is | sinking | In the golden | West, | Night will soon be | folding | All the world to | rest.

Now the Sun Is Sinking

Andante

7

PRIMO
Ding-Dong, Bell

Ding-dong, bell! Pus-sy's in the well! Who put her in? Lit-tle John-nie Green.

London Bridge Is Falling Down

English Folk Tune

Lon - don Bridge is fall - ing down, fall - ing down, fall - ing down,

Lon - don Bridge is fall - ing down, My fair la - dy.____

Now the Sun Is Sinking

Now the Sun Is Sinking

Now the sun is sinking In the golden West: Night will soon be folding All the world to rest.

SECONDO

Evening

German Folk Tune

Oh! How qui - et is the eve - ning When the sun is grow - ing red. And the birds are chirp-ing soft - ly, Get-ting read - y for bed.

The Rose Is Red

If I Were A Tiny Elfin

Bohemian Melody

mp If I were a ti - ny el - fin Just as high as a fly, ——

I would creep in - to a flow - er There to lie.

Little Jack Horner

(Pupil)

mp Lit - tle Jack Hor - ner Sat in a cor - ner Eat - ing his Christ - mas pie. ——

He put in his thumb And pulled out a plum And said what a good boy am I! ——

48574

SECONDO

Hush-A-Bye Baby

Andante

Christmas Song

Andante con moto

French Folk Tune

Hush-A-Bye Baby

Christmas Song

French Folk Tune

SECONDO
The Bells Of London

English Folk Tune

Four And Twenty Blackbirds

The Bells Of London

English Folk Tune

Four And Twenty Blackbirds

Minuet

Bohemian Folk Tune

My Country, 'tis of Thee

Happy New Year

French Folk Tune

Cashmere Song

Joseph and Mary

Old English Carol

Cashmere Song

Joseph and Mary

Nineteen Birds

Old French Air

Nineteen Birds

Old French Air

Giroflè, giroflà

French Folk Tune

Bohemian Song

Giroflè, giroflà

French Folk Tune

Bohemian Song

48574

Scale of D

Luther's Hymn

German Chorale

PRIMO

Scale of D

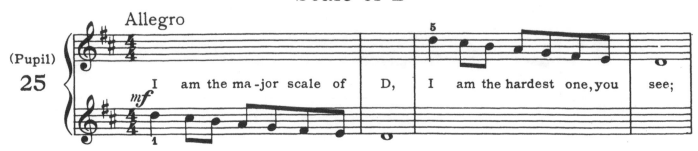

Luther's Hymn

German Chorale

48574

Plaisir d'Amour

Martini

The First Noël

Traditional Melody

Plaisir d'Amour

Martini

The First Noël

Traditional Melody

The Cruel Rose

Old French Air

Bohemian Dance

The Cruel Rose

Old French Air

Allegretto

(Pupil)
29

Bohemian Dance

Allegro con brio

(Pupil)
30

Russian Hymn

The Seagull

Irish Folk Tune

Russian Hymn

The Seagull

Irish Folk Tune

Frère Jacques

French Folk Tune

The Ballad of King Henry

Old English Melody

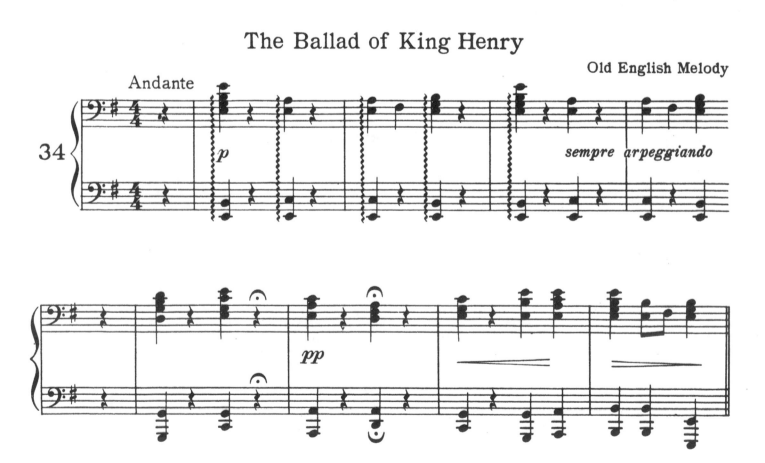

Frère Jacques

French Folk Tune

The Ballad of King Henry

Old English Melody

1.

O, where have you been wandering, King Henry, my son?
O, where have you been wandering, my pretty one?
I've been to my sweetheart: mother, make my bed soon,
For I'm sick to the heart, and would fain lay me down.

2.

And what did your sweetheart give you, King Henry, my son?
And what did your sweetheart give you, my pretty one?
She fried me some paddocks: mother, make my bed soon,
For I'm sick to the heart, and would fain lay me down.

3.

And what will you leave your sweetheart, King Henry, my son?
O what will you leave your sweetheart, my pretty one?
A rope for to hang her, mother! make my bed soon,
For I'm sick to the heart, and would fain lay me down.

The Wraggle-Taggle Gipsies

English Folk Tune

Canon in A minor

The Wraggle-Taggle Gipsies

English Folk Tune

Allegro

(Pupil)
35

1.
It was late last night when my lord came home
   Enquiring for his a-lady, O!
The servants said, on every hand,
   She's gone with the wraggle-taggle gipsies, O!
2.
O, he rode high, and he rode low,
   He rode through woods and copses, too,
Until he came to an open field,
   And there he espied his a-lady, O!

3.
What makes you leave your house and land?
   What makes you leave your money, O?
What makes you leave your new wedded lord
   To go with the wraggle-taggle gipsies, O?
4.
O what care I for my house and my land?
   What care I for my money, O?
What care I for my new wedded lord?
   I'm off with the wraggle-taggle gipsies, O!

Canon in A minor

Andante

(Pupil)
36

SECONDO

Jock o' Hazeldean

Scotch Air

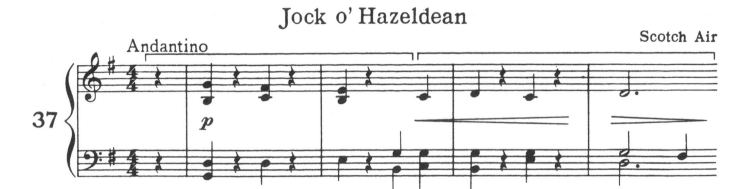

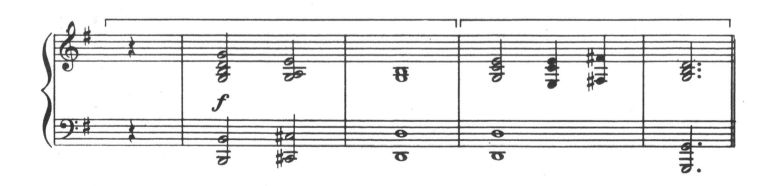

Jock o' Hazeldean

Scotch Air

1.

Why weep ye by the tide, ladye,
  Why weep ye by the tide?
I'll wed ye to my youngest son,
  And ye shall be his bride.
And ye shall be his bride, ladye,
  Sae comely to be seen —
But aye she loot the tears doun fa',
  For Jock o' Hazeldean.

2.

The kirk was decked at morning tide,
  The taper glimmered fair,
The priest and bridegroom wait the bride,
  And dame and knight are there.
They sought her baith by bower and ha',
  The lady was not seen;
She's o'er the border and awa'
  Wi' Jock o' Hazeldean.

48574

SECONDO

Dutch Tune

Bergerette

Old French Air

Dutch Tune

Bergerette

Old French Air

48574

Parting Song

Old Manx Tune

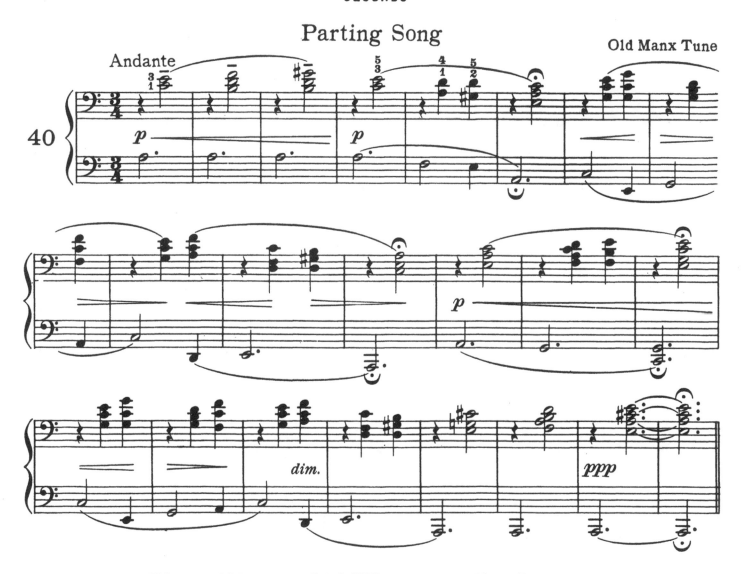

There Was an Old Woman, as I've Heard Tell

English Folk Tune

Parting Song

Old Manx Tune

There Was an Old Woman, as I've Heard Tell

English Folk Tune

Winter, Farewell

German Folk Tune

The North Wind Doth Blow

J. W. Elliott

Hot Cross Buns

English Folk Tune

SECONDO

Hippity Hop!

English Folk Tune

Creole Song

Hippity Hop!

English Folk Tune

Creole Song

Leezie Lindsay

Scotch Air

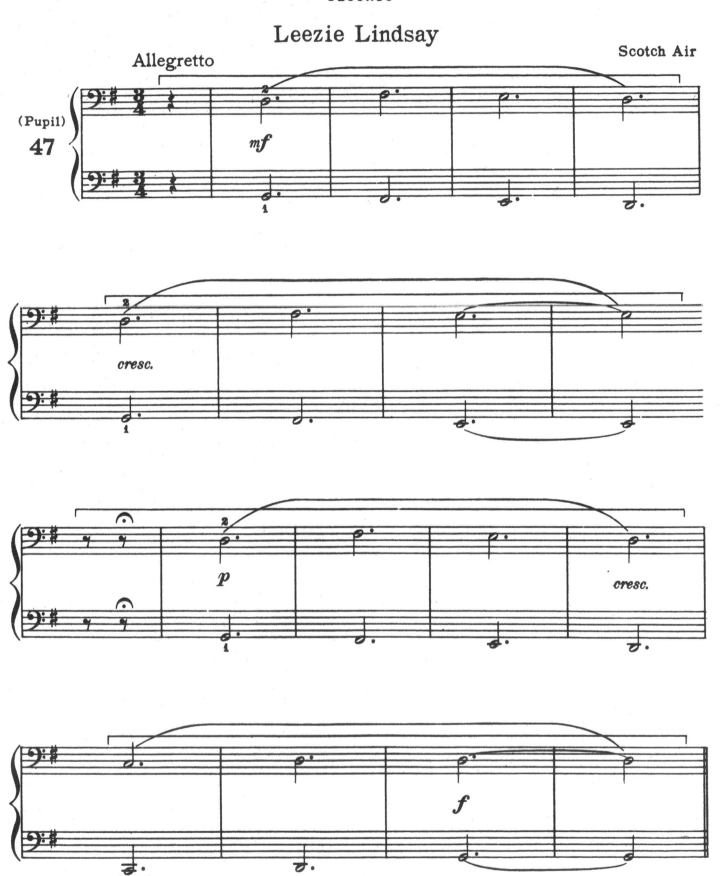

Leezie Lindsay

Allegretto

Scotch Air

47

1.

Will ye gang to the Hielan's, Leezie Lindsay?
    Will ye gang to the Hielan's wi' me?
Will ye gang to the Hielan's, Leezie Lindsay,
    My bride an' my darlin' to be?

2.

To gang to the Hielan's wi' you, sir,
    I dinna ken how that may be,
For I ken na' the land that ye live in,
    Nor ken I the lad I'm gaun wi'.

3.

O Leezie lass, ye maun ken little,
    If sae be that ye dinna ken me;
My name is Lord Ronald MacDonald,
    A chieftan o' high degree.

4.

She has kilted her coats o' green satin,
    She has kilted them up to the knee,
And she's off wi' Lord Ronald MacDonald,
    His bride an' his darlin' to be.

48574

SECONDO

The Chimes

French Folk Tune

Polish Dance

Irish Tune

The Chimes

French Folk Tune

Polish Dance

Irish Tune

The Day of Christmas

Andante con moto

English Folk Tune

Sleep, Belovèd, Sleep

Andantino

German Folk Tune

(Pupil)

The Day of Christmas

English Folk Tune

Sleep, Belovèd, Sleep

German Folk Tune

Exaudet's Minuet

Cradle-Song

German Melody

Exaudet's Minuet

Cradle-Song

German Melody

Holy Night

German Folk Tune

Christ Was Born on Christmas Day

German Folk Tune

Holy Night

Andante con moto

German Folk Tune

Christ Was Born on Christmas Day

Allegretto

German Folk Tune

(Pupil)

56

Schubert Waltz

Spring Song
English Folk Tune

Schubert Waltz

Spring Song

Winter

Austrian Hymn

PRIMO

Winter

Bohemian Folk Tune

Andantino

59

Austrian Hymn

Maestoso

Josef Haydn

(Pupil)
60

48574

Beside Thy Cradle Here I Stand

J. S. Bach

PRIMO

Beside Thy Cradle Here I Stand

J. S. Bach

SECONDO

What Tongue Can Tell Thy Greatness, Lord?

Old Chorale

48574

PRIMO

What Tongue Can Tell Thy Greatness, Lord?

Old Chorale

48574

FOREWORD TO THE 1983 REVISED EDITION

It is time to prepare a new edition of the First Duet Book. In undertaking this, we have tried to maintain in every way the musical character of the book as originally written. Duets for pupil and teacher are of value in arousing and keeping alive the child's interest because they permit him/her to participate in making real music long before he/she would otherwise be able to do so.

The aim of this book is to parallel approximately the grading and material of the First Solo Book, which has also recently been revised. Many teachers, however, have felt a need for simpler pieces at the beginning. Therefore we have added some easier duets, arranged from other Diller-Quaile material. They should give the student a feeling of accomplishment and pleasure before attempting the more difficult ones.

The first four duets are confined to the few notes centered around middle C and can be learned in that familiar range but played an octave higher when the teacher's part is added.

We hope that this new edition will increase the value of the book especially for those who feel playing duets is an invaluable experience for sight reading.

Dorothy Weed
Teacher at the Diller-Quaile School of Music
since 1922
Music Director 1955-1972

Robert Fraley
Teacher at the Diller-Quaile School of Music
since 1961
Director since 1972

PREFACE TO THE ORIGINAL EDITION

The First Solo Book and First Duet Book have two objects:

(1)   To provide, from the beginning of the child's piano study, material of permanent *musical value* which shall serve as a basis for the development of his taste.

With the exception of a few preliminary exercises, all the pieces in these Books are either folk-tunes that have been sung by generations of children, or classics that should be part of every child's musical experience.

We believe that the child can be interested very early in his musical career in different styles of composition so we have used folk-tunes of many nations, modal tunes, chorales, etc., including, from the beginning, pieces of irregular metrical structure, i.e., not confined to the usual two- and four-measure phrase-lengths.

Music of this character cannot be heard too often, and we feel sure that the teacher as well as the pupil will appreciate the absence of original "teaching pieces."

(2)   To provide a plentiful selection of pieces of real musical interest so carefully graded, both musically and technically, that the child is stimulated but not overtaxed.

In the First Solo Book, the pieces are printed only in the more common major and minor keys, but the child should be taught to transpose these pieces into all keys. This insures a familiarity with the keyboard and a sense of tone-relationship that is invaluable.

The necessary foundation for the artistic playing of any instrument is a musical ear. Pianoforte-playing in itself cannot, by any means, be relied upon to furnish this, as the attention of the child is necessarily focused upon the overcoming of technical difficulties. Therefore, it is recommended that the child be given a large experience of music before he begins the study of an instrument. Just as language is learned first by hearing and then by speaking and reading, so music should be learned by experiencing it before learning to read or to perform on an instrument. Singing is the natural mode of musical expression and learning to sing a large number of good songs "by ear" will greatly broaden the child's musical horizon. When he thus has had actual experience of music, he will be more interested in learning to read and to play.

ANGELA DILLER
ELIZABETH QUAILE

Solo and Duet Books

For the Piano

**Collected and Harmonized,
Edited and Fingered
by ANGELA DILLER
and ELIZABETH QUAILE**

FIRST SOLO BOOK
New Edition

SECOND SOLO BOOK
New Edition

THIRD SOLO BOOK

FOURTH SOLO BOOK

FIRST DUET BOOK
New Edition
SECOND DUET BOOK
New Edition

THIRD DUET BOOK

G. SCHIRMER, Inc.

DISTRIBUTED BY

HAL•LEONARD®
CORPORATION
7777 W. BLUEMOUND RD. P.O. BOX 13819 MILWAUKEE, WI 53213

T0050711

ED. 3438

Composer's notes – Taylor Made

Style & History

'Taylor Made' is a gentle folk tune with a simple melody and chord structure. Have a listen to **Paul Simon**'s 'Bridge Over Troubled Water', **Bob Dylan**'s 'Blowin' in the Wind' or **James Taylor**'s 'Carolina in My Mind' to get an idea of the modern folk style.

Harmony

The scale below can be used for soloing in this tune. Play the scale then sing the scale, then play it again! This will help you to get in touch with the notes you will be using. Make use of the blue note now and again for a touch of 'spice' if you like.

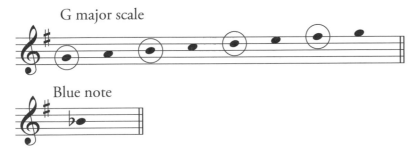

The circled notes are the 'stronger' notes of the scale – they are the notes that make up the chord relevant to this scale. If you want your solo to sound 'safe' and 'grounded' use these notes, if you want it to sound a little more distant from the chords, try using the notes that are not circled.

Rhythm

The rhythm below may seem tricky; listen to the demo track whilst looking at the part. This way you will start to associate how this rhythm looks on paper with what you can hear.

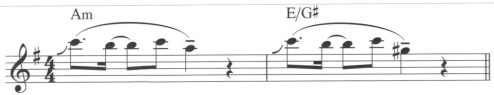

Tips & Projects

As 'Taylor Made' has a reflective quality, it would make musical sense to leave plenty of space within your solo.

Below are the chords for letter E, try adding these suggested notes:

These notes are, again, the stronger notes of each chord. They are the roots and 3rds. If this seems tricky, to begin with you can use the tune again (from letter C).

The backing track fades out towards the end so try to match this in your playing by getting softer and using more space.

Taylor Made

Rob Hughes and Paul Harvey

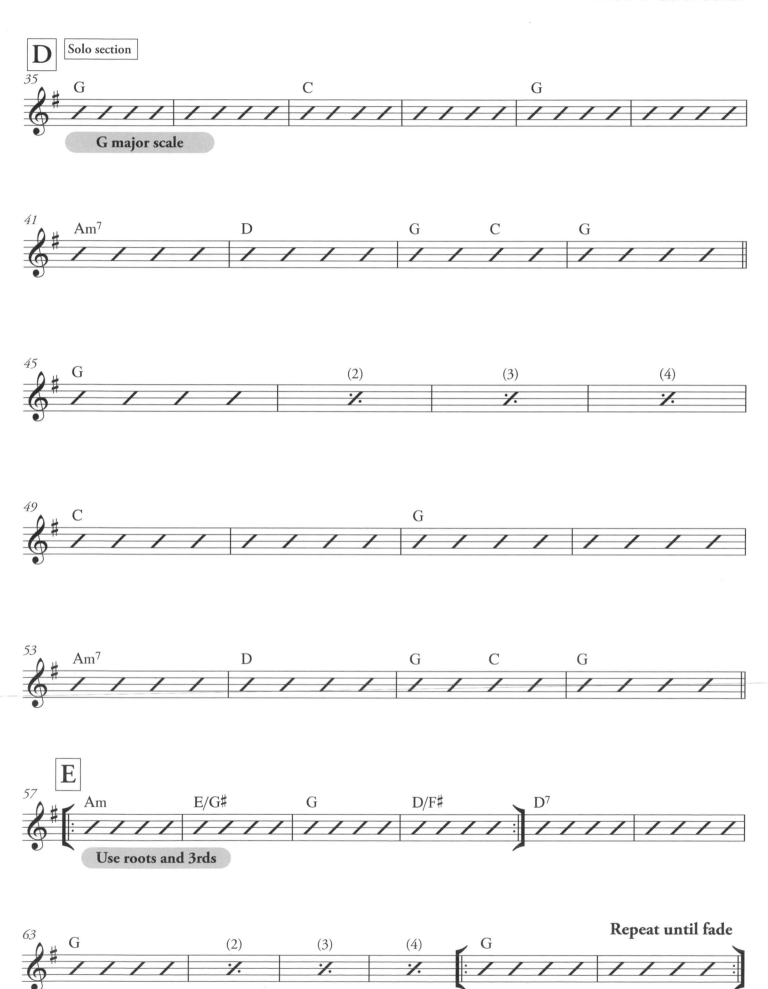

Composer's notes – Detroit Cowboy

Style & History

'Detroit Cowboy' is a Motown-style tune. Motown was a record label started by **Berry Gordy**, **Jr.** in Detroit and was sometimes referred to as the 'hits factory'. They had a winning pool of musicians and writers who contributed to the majority of the songs.

The Motown sound consisted of prominent and interesting bass lines and the use of call-and-response type melodies. Brass and string sections were also important, as was the use of the tambourine.

Some of the numerous Motown artists include: **Mary Wells**, **The Supremes**, **The Four Tops**, **The Jackson 5**, **Boyz II Men** and **The Commodores**. Listen to **The Temptations** tune 'Ain't Too Proud to Beg' to get a flavour of the classic Motown sound.

Harmony

You can use the major scale and blue note below to solo with in this tune.

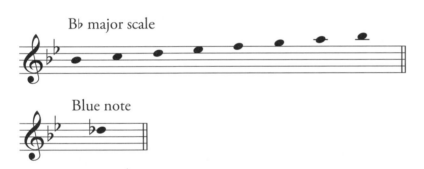

Rhythm

This next rhythm looks worse than it actually is. Put simply, the tied notes add up to a crotchet but are not played on the beat. The best way to work on this rhythm is to look at the part whilst listening to the demo track. Do this a few times and you will soon get used to how to play this phrase.

Tips & Projects

'Detroit Cowboy' has a 16-bar solo at letter D. It can be difficult to solo for a set amount of bars and then return back to the tune at the correct time (letter E). To begin with, don't improvise the first time you get to letter D, instead count the 16 bars and listen out for clues on the backing track as to where you need to come back in.

When you do solo over this section, it should then be second nature to you when the 16 bars are up.

The solo section at letter G is a chance to really go for it. You do not need to worry about coming back in as the tune doesn't return.

Detroit Cowboy

Rob Hughes and Paul Harvey

Composer's notes – Musique Rom

Style & History

'Musique Rom' is a jazz tune and, as it's in 3 time, could be referred to as a 'jazz waltz'. The head is a straightforward melody that can be played as written, perhaps with a lightly decorated (ad lib.) version on the Dal Segno.

Another example of a jazz waltz is 'My Favourite Things' by **Rodgers** and **Hammerstein**. This featured in the musical *The Sound of Music* and has become a firm favourite for many jazz musicians over the years.

Harmony

Below is a pentatonic scale which can be used for the entire solo. To add interest and tension, try adding in the

blue note below. Remember to pass from this note to a 'safe', main chord note quickly.

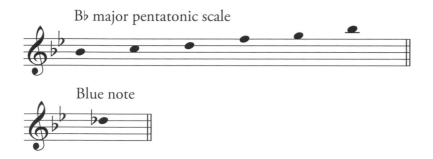

Rhythm

In your solo, borrow some of the different rhythmic ideas from the head such as bars 5, 13 and 27. This will give your solo a sense of coherence. You can use them as

they are, or develop them by perhaps swapping the order of the pitches, or maybe omitting a rest or two.

Tips & Projects

After working on the pentatonic scale above, use the following as a suggestion for the solo section:

This example is for the first chord in the solo section. It outlines the most important notes of the chord: the root, 3rd and 7th.

Below are the notes to use over the second chord in the solo. Again it's the root, 3rd and 7th of the chord. Practise playing these chord notes with the backing

track. Once you can achieve this with ease, play the notes in a different order. Next, alternate between using the pentatonic scale and these chord notes.

13

Musique Rom

Rob Hughes

Composer's notes – Funk 24

Style & History

'Funk 24', as the title suggests, is a funk tune! The background to this genre is described in the text for 'What's in the Bag?' on page 4. One band who are synonymous with funk are **The Average White Band**. If you listen to one of their most famous tracks, 'Pick Up The Pieces', you may hear some of the influences that 'Funk 24' has drawn on. To really get into the funky style, pay particular attention to the written dynamics and articulations.

Harmony

Use the pentatonic scale below for improvising, any of these notes will work well in your solo. Start your solo with a sense of space, don't try to cram in all the notes at once otherwise you will have nothing left to play towards the end. Think about the solo as a conversation – when you meet someone you don't normally speak at 100 mph, so apply this rationale to your solo.

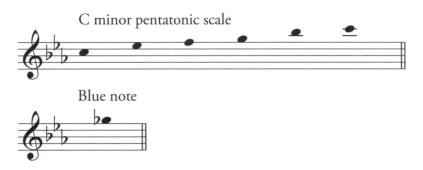

Rhythm

This piece has lots of funky rhythms. Develop your own riffs based on the rhythm of the first four bars, shown below. For example, start by playing the riff a few times until you have memorized it, then copy the rhythms but change two or three of the pitches.

Once you have mastered this, alter one or two of the rhythms so that you are gradually moving away from the original idea. This is a great way to start a progression that you can build on through your solo.

Tips & Projects

Work out how to play the 8-bar solo which starts at bar 17 (demonstrated on the CD). Once you can play it from memory, have a go at writing it out.

Funk 24

Rob Hughes and Paul Harvey

Composer's notes – Hold On

Style & History

'Hold On' is composed in the 'Philly Soul' style. Philly (or Philadelphia) Soul, has funk and jazz influences, often with elaborate instrumental arrangements. Those well known for this style include: **McFadden** and **Whitehead** ('Ain't No Stoppin' Us Now'), **Jackie Wilson**, **The Three Degrees** and **Grover Washington**, **Jr**.

This is a ballad, so be sure to work on being expressive with your dynamics – this will help to get across the melodic intentions of the tune. Play with confidence, but not too loudly.

Harmony

If you make your first eight bars spacious, the solo will have time to build up gently. The main scale to solo with is shown below, together with a blue note.

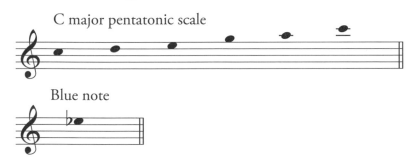

Once you are comfortable with the pentatonic scale, look at the chord changes at bars 45 and 47. The chord is shifting from major to minor and it would also be favourable to include the major 7th going to the minor 6th. Here are the strong chord notes:

Rhythm

At letter D there is a rhythm indicated in the part, if you included or referenced it in your improvisation it will sound great! Solo for the first eight bars then play what is written at letter D for three bars. Then try using just the rhythm from letter D, but changing the pitches to whatever you prefer.

Tips & Projects

This tune uses 'acciaccaturas' throughout to achieve a soulful vibe. They are brief in duration, played as though 'brushed' on the way to the principal note (which receives virtually all of its notated length).

They are also sometimes described as 'crushed' notes, which may help you in tackling this type of ornament. Have a go at writing a 4-bar phrase using an acciaccatura at least once.

Hold On

Rob Hughes and Paul Harvey

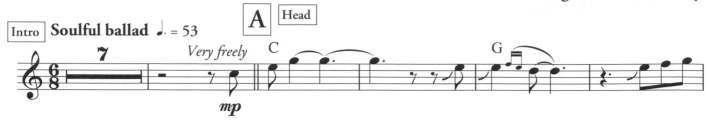

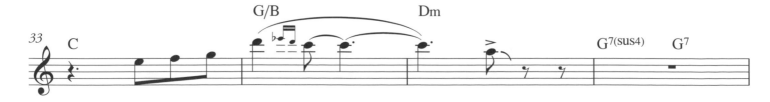

Composer's notes – Mystery

Style & History

'Mystery' is a reggae tune. Reggae is a music genre that originated from Jamaica in the late 1960s. Two strong rhythmic devices are often used with this style of music: the second and fourth beats of each bar are usually accented (as played by the guitar chords on this track) and the bass often leaves the first beat of the bar silent or tied over from the previous bar. Harmonically, the music is usually very simple, sometimes the entire song will have no more than one or two chords. These simple repetitive devices add to reggae's sometimes-hypnotic effect. Listen to 'I Shot the Sheriff' by **Bob Marley** or 'Red Red Wine' by **UB40** for examples of great reggae tunes.

Harmony

It's worth noting that this piece shifts between minor sections, letters A, C, D and F, and major sections, letters B, E, G and H.

The blues scale below can be used for soloing.

Rhythm

We have several crotchet triplets in this tune; this involves playing three crotchets in the time of two. A common mistake is to rush the last crotchet, so make sure that they are all even and laid back, which will fit in with the easy-going reggae character. Listen carefully to the demo track to get the idea.

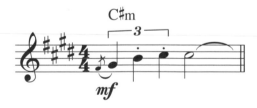

Tips & Projects

The feel of the piece is quite relaxed, so convey this by letting your solo be open, unhurried and spacious. As a starting point, take some quotes (short melodic ideas) from the tune itself.

At letter F you can hear the organ playing simple phrases on the backing track – as an exercise, try copying or answering them.

On the repeat of letter G the backings come in again – work on playing around them at first (play in between the phrases) until your solo becomes more intense, at which point you may decide that you want to play over them.

7 Mystery

Rob Hughes and Paul Harvey

Composer's notes – Busticate

Style & History

'Busticate' is quasi-orchestral with a repetitive, rhythmic accompaniment and an angular melody. One of the best exponents of this type of music is **Mike Mower** – a British-based saxophonist and composer who has written for the saxophone group **Itchy Fingers**. This genre bridges the gap between jazz and classical music.

Harmony

The solo section starts at letter C, where you can use the pentatonic scale below. Add in the blue note for colour.

F minor pentatonic scale

Blue note

At letter D the chord sequence changes. You can still use the pentatonic scale but at bar 40, use the arpeggio below. Practise this without any backing at first – play three bars of the pentatonic scale and then one bar of the arpeggio.

D♭ major arpeggio

At letter E the chord sequence changes again. Use the pentatonic scale for the first two bars of letter E. At bar 43, try using the major 7th arpeggio (below).

E♭ major 7th arpeggio

Rhythm

Perhaps the trickiest aspect of this tune is rhythm. To accomplish this you will need to be rhythmically very strict with yourself and have a 'rock solid' inner pulse – you must always know where beat one is!

Tips & Projects

Here's an example of a 'blue note in action'. Come up with some variations, and include them in your solo.

Busticate

Rob Hughes

Composer's notes – Nital

Style & History

'Nital' is written in a Latin-jazz style (a general term given to jazz music with Latin-American rhythmic influences). In comparison with traditional jazz, Latin jazz uses straight quavers, rather than swung.

To get acquainted with the sound, listen to 'The Girl from Ipanema', a well-known Latin tune. Play 'Nital' with a gentle volume, save your more energetic playing for the end of the piece.

Harmony

Use this pentatonic scale and blue note at letter D:

Bb major pentatonic scale

Blue note

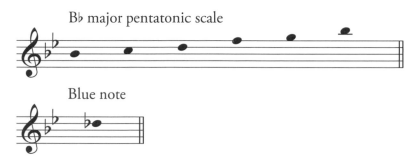

At bar 45 we have a diminished chord, this features a flattened 3rd and 5th, and a diminished 7th.

A dim arpeggio

At letter G, use the pentatonic scale again, when you get to bar 85 change to the major scale below:

G major scale

For bars 95–96 use an Eb major arpeggio.

Rhythm

Play the rhythm shown here (from bar 20) with the same vigour as the guitar displays on the backing track from bar 32. Your playing needs to be very tight and crisp.

Tips & Projects

Write out a solo for the first four bars of letter D. If possible, incorporate the arpeggio idea from the harmony section at bar 45. As this is the start of your solo, make sure it's not too busy.

Nital

Rob Hughes and Paul Harvey

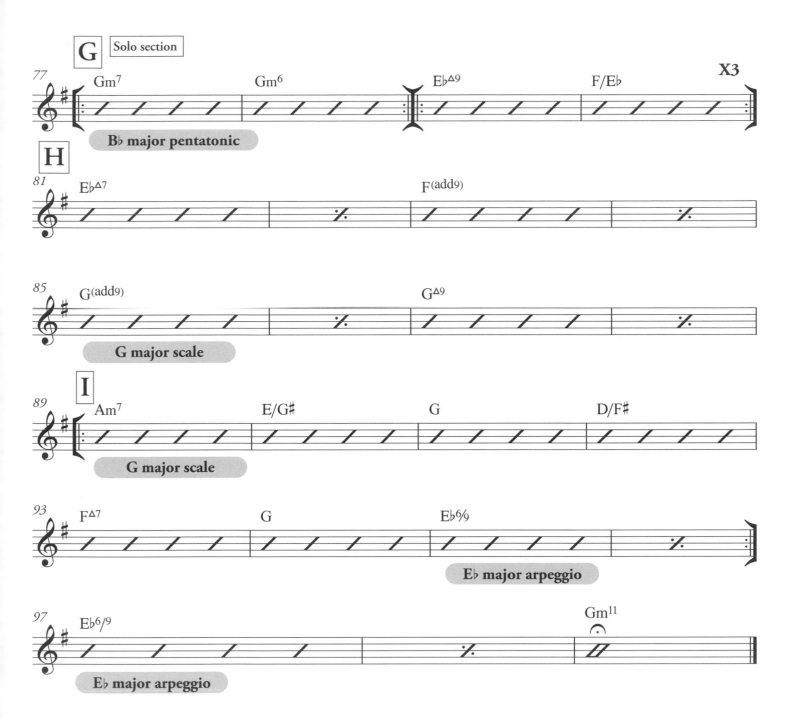

Track Listing

1. What's in the Bag?
2. Taylor Made
3. Detroit Cowboy
4. Musique Rom
5. Funk 24
6. Hold On
7. Mystery
8. Busticate
9. Nital

Tracks 4 and 8 written by Rob Hughes, all other tracks written by Rob Hughes and Paul Harvey.

As an additional bonus, you will find MP3 demonstration versions for all the other instruments in this series (see below for accessing MP3s). These can be used to further your appreciation of how different musicians, on a variety of instruments, approach the same improvisational material.

Recording Acknowledgments

Soloists (demo tracks):

Alto sax, Flute and Tenor sax – **Rob Hughes**

Clarinet – **Richard Beesley**

Guitar – **Paul Harvey**

Trombone – **Barnaby Dickinson**

Trumpet – **Graeme Flowers**

Violin – **Chris Haigh**

Backing tracks:

Alto sax, Bass Clarinet, Clarinet, Flute, Soprano sax and Tenor sax – **Rob Hughes**

Guitars, Bass and all programming – **Paul Harvey**

Recorded and mixed by **Rob Hughes** and **Paul Harvey** at Pocket Studios, June-October 2010

Using the CD

On the enclosed CD you will find demonstration versions of each tune, with the instrumental line played in full, as well as backing tracks for you to play along with.

Accessing the CD backing tracks:

The backing tracks are regular CD audio tracks. If used with a *conventional CD player*, only the backing tracks will play.

To play the backing tracks *on a computer*, first open a media player such as iTunes or Windows media player.

Insert the 'Free to Solo' CD – the backing tracks should appear after a few moments and can either be played or imported, as you would with any other audio CD.

Accessing the MP3 demonstration tracks:

Insert the 'Free to Solo' CD into a computer, navigate to your CD drive and click open. Find the folder marked 'MP3 demos'. Inside the folder you will find a folder for your instrument, you can then copy these demonstration versions to your computer's media player.